The official guide to Compact D...
from Philips Interactive Media Systems

Introducing

CD-I

PHILIPS IMS

ADDISON-WESLEY
PUBLISHING
COMPANY

Wokingham, England · Reading, Massachusetts · Menlo Park, California · New York
Don Mills, Ontario · Amsterdam · Bonn · Sydney · Singapore
Tokyo · Madrid · San Juan · Milan · Paris · Mexico City · Seoul · Taipei

Many of the designations used by manufacturers and sellers to distinguish their
products are claimed as trademarks. Addison-Wesley has made every attempt to
supply trademark information about manufacturers and their products mentioned in
this book. A list of the trademark designations and their owners appears on p.viii.

Cover designed by Chris Eley
and printed by The Riverside Printing Co (Reading) Ltd
Film separations by Keene Graphics Bureau
Printed in Great Britain by William Clowes, Beccles, Suffolk

First printed 1992

ISBN 0-201-62748-5

Acknowledgments
Philips and Addison-Wesley would like to acknowledge TMS, Computer Authors for
producing this text, Zap Art, Bernard Gudynas and Peter Gudynas for the art
direction, layout design and illustrations. With the invaluable assistance of Nick
Lloyd (photoshop techno) and Kevin White (typo techno). Thanks to David Collier for
initial concept work and introducing Zap Art to CD-I. We would also like to thank
the many reviewers who have contributed valuable comments as the project
progressed and especially Mike Everall (Interlight Productions), Clive Shepherd (EPIC
Interactive), Paul Norris (Binary Vision) and Dr David Matthewson.

British Library Cataloguing in Publication Data
A catalogue record for this book is available from the British Library.

Library of Congress Cataloging in Publication Data

To coincide with the worldwide availability of CD-I, the first of a series of authoritative publications on this technology is being published.

This, the first book in the series, is aimed at a broad audience from interactive producers and designers to all those interested in the applications of CD-I technology. It is non-technical and aims to give an overview of how the CD-I standard for electronic publishing will impact on offices, schools and homes around the world.

Since the first release of the CD-I Green Book specification in November 1988 to the licensees, we have come a long way. Numerous professional projects have been started in the United States, Japan and Europe with CD-I applications in museums; the pharmaceutical and chemical industries; at universities and in the high street.

A large number of publishers have developed the first CD-I consumer titles along with Philips Interactive Media of America. Similar developments are now taking place in Europe and Japan. In all these markets, consortia have been set up with major publishers, producers, consumer electronics hardware manufacturers and retailers as members.

CD-I revolutionises publishing of all kinds of material: music, text, images, film and data and adds capabilities not possible with traditional publishing methods. The present titles covering music, family entertainment, children, sports, reference and knowledge, self-help and 'how-to' subjects, are the best proof that this revolution has begun.

We firmly believe that the basic conditions for the success of CD-I have been fulfilled and that this book will give an excellent introduction should you wish to take part in this exciting business and entertainment opportunity.

Gaston A. J. Bastiaens,
Director,
Philips Interactive Media Systems,
Eindhoven, The Netherlands

April 1992

CONTENTS

DEVELOPMENT AND PRODUCTION

CASE STUDY

GLOSSARY

INDEX

Photo Acknowledgements
The photographs on the following pages are produced with permission and
©The Hulton-Deutsch Collection: 12 and 23 (The ape, film still from 'Captive Wild
Woman'), 15-16, 135, and 137 (Charlie Chaplin and Marilyn Monroe), 20 (Boris
Karloff as Frankenstein), 23 (Water Music and Mick Jagger), 25 (The show, Alice In
Wonderland), 29-30 (Charlie Chapin in 'Modern Times'), 31 (Pavarotti), 37-38
('Cinerama'), 52 (Laurence Olivier and Salvador Dali), 60 (Carmen Miranda),
63 (The ape), 64 (Marilyn Monroe and Pavorotti), 69-70 (Gary Lineker and Fred
Astaire) 77(Beatles), and 81-82 (Robbie the robot, Orson Welles as Citizen Kane
and Liza Minnelli).

The photographs on the following pages are produced with permission
© Mike Smallcombe: 1 and 4 (Power Woman), 44 (CD-EYE) and 85 (Margaritte).

The photographs on pages 27-28 are produced with permission and © Kodak Ltd

All photomontage illustrations created by © Zap Art

INTRODUCING CD-I

E-234 452 --.LTT8272007 2RDF

Question: What do the following
scenes have in common?

4

7

3

Ex 1

Ex 2

Ex 3

Ex 4

Ex 5

Ex 6

Ex 7

"Linear television is closing down"
Douglas Adams

Ex 8

CARTOON JUKEBOX

A seven year old girl sitting in front of a television at her school chooses a cartoon she wants to watch. Using a remote control, she colours in the first frame of the cartoon, selects some words for the accompanying song and then presses a button. The television plays back the cartoon with her colours and words. Whilst working through the options she has been learning elementary arithmetic.

INTRODUCING **CD-I**

3

BODYWORKS

A man concerned with his weight looks at a television. The scene is a health centre. A receptionist asks him his weight, age and blood pressure. He then chooses whether he wants to see a health advisor or have a work out. He decides to have a work out. He chooses one of six types of exercise and an instructress in a blue leotard allocates him to one of thirty possible fitness levels and works out a series of exercises for him. He enters the doors of the gymnasium and the instructress takes him through series of aerobics. Later, a little fitter, he visits the health advisor and is given a diet plan which will help him to tackle his weight problem.

4

Ex 3

A couple planning a tour of the United States are trying to decide whether to visit the Smithsonian Institution in Washington. They enter the museum and look around it. At various stages they decide that they want to see only objects from a certain historical period or associated with a certain person. Sometimes they just want to go in directions that take their fancy. They can see paintings and objects, even walk around sculptures. They can read informative pieces of text, and then go to entirely different parts of the museum. They do not leave their living room.

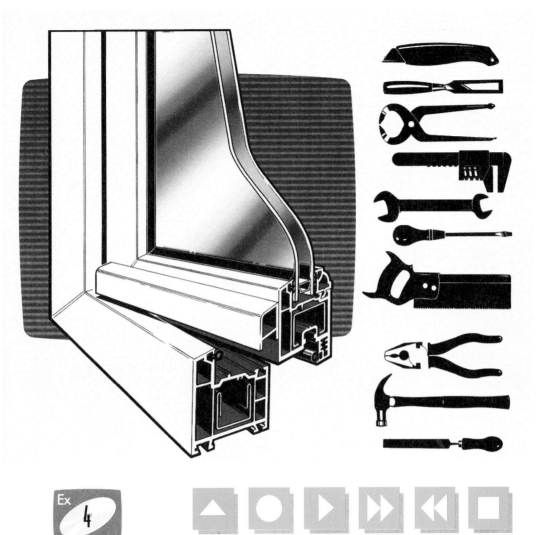

Ex
4

A man in a large Do-It-Yourself store sees a television. He walks up and touches a panel on the screen. The television introduces him to the complexities of double glazing. He finds out about his requirements and what he needs to do to satisfy them. At each stage he is able to find exactly what information he needs about double glazing systems. No-one is pressuring him and he is able to explore all the possibilities he wants. When he is satisfied, he goes to the assistant of the store and orders precisely what he needs without any fuss.

Ex **5**

A learner driver wishing to learn rules about stopping distances selects first a speed, then road conditions and then does an emergency stop. The car crashes spectacularly into the back of an articulated truck. The driver passes a handkerchief over his brow. Luckily the whole incident only takes place on a television screen.

75ft   **175ft**   **315ft**

30   **50**   **70**
mph   mph   mph

INTRODUCING **CD-I**

7

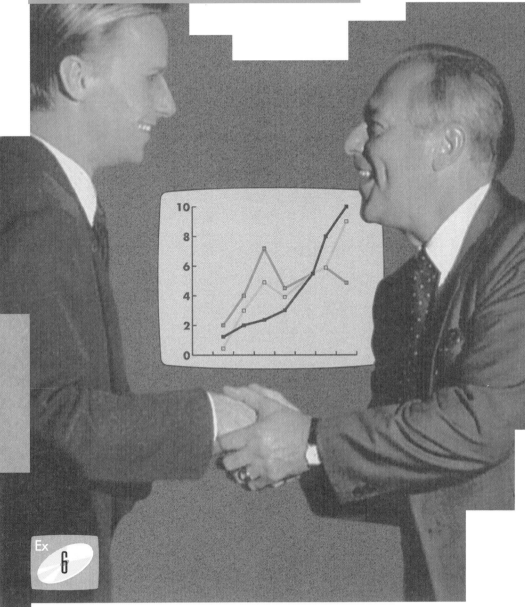

Ex
6

A management consultant wants to make a presentation about the services his company offers for a trade exhibition using material he has written and designed himself. Instead of slides and poor graphics, he has a smoothly flowing series of images, accompanied by music and text. Potential clients are impressed by the professionalism of the show. He is able to throw away his indigestion tablets and concentrate on giving people useful advice.

8

Ex **7**

A family is driving up a street in what seems to be an ordinary small town. On one side of the street is a gothic mansion, next to it a suburban house. Opposite is a small side street of workers' cottages. Further down the road are the Taj Mahal, a twisted hollow oak tree and a huge and mysterious earth mound. Their automobile engine begins to splutter and they run out of gas. They have to choose where they are going to ask for help.

Edgar Allan Poe, a little the worse for wear, beckons to them from the porch of the gothic mansion. Agatha Christie twitches the lace curtains of the suburban house, but the youngest child is attracted by the swarthy gnome who sits puffing his acorn pipe unconcernedly in front of the hollow oak tree.

The gnome welcomes them into his leafy home. They try not to be distracted by the screams from the gothic mansion or the sight of the man in the tightly-belted trenchcoat burying an awkward bundle in his garden, or the smell of Indian cooking or the sound of brass bands from the cobbled Victorian street or the muffled trumpet fanfares from the army of the dead entombed in the earth mound.

In their search for gas they spend many hours in the labyrinth of tunnels beneath the earth. It seems as if they will never escape the frightful fakir or the terrifying clog dancers. Suddenly it is time for bed. They open a large pair of bronze doors and enter a concert hall where the Berlin Philharmonic conducted by Otto Klemperer, is playing a slow tempo version of Brahms' Lullaby. They are unable to prevent themselves from falling into a deep sleep in which they make the awful realisation that up until this point they have been awake...

SOAP OPERA

Ex 8 **The** Bronzino family sit watching The Brownstones, a soap about the everyday life of New York folk, on their television. In this episode Aggie Brownstone has been mugged between Fifth and Sixth Avenues. Mr Bronzino can't remember where Fifth and Sixth Avenue are. Mrs Bronzino has an idea that one of them is a famous shopping street. Archie Bronzino, their son can't remember who Aggie Browstone is. Is she Nathan Brownstone's unmarried daughter, or did she marry into the Brownstones in an earlier episode which they missed because the scheduling was changed?

Angelica Bronzino quickly rifles through a rack of what appear to be CD discs and brings out a disc called Brownstones Fact File. She puts it into a slot beneath the television screen and, while still watching the soap opera, they are able to use their remote control to dedicate half of their screen to maps of New York and potted biographies of the main characters and the actors who play them. Intense peace reigns in the Bronzino household.

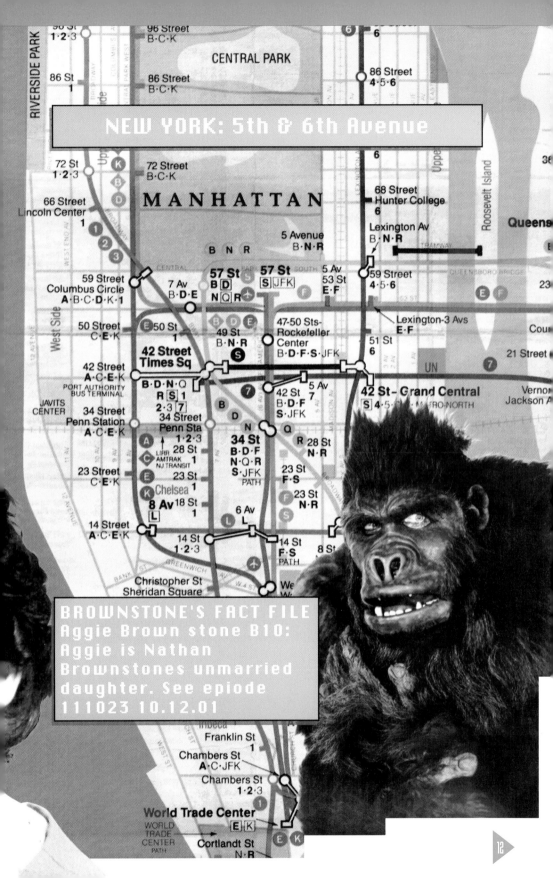

NEW YORK: 5th & 6th Avenue

BROWNSTONE'S FACT FILE
Aggie Brown stone B10:
Aggie is Nathan
Brownstones unmarried
daughter. See epiode
111023 10.12.01

Answer: A CD-I disc

INFO
i

SETTINGS

MEMORY

DIM

OPEN

E-234 452 --.LTT82272007 2RDF

INTERACTIVE TELEVISION

CD-I stands for Compact Disc - Interactive. A CD-I disc looks exactly like an ordinary CD audio disc. It has the familiar plastic coating and rainbow sheen, but it differs from digital audio discs in one vital respect: you can put it in a CD-I player, play a programme on your television and interact with it. Interactive television is a new concept. Ordinary television and video players meet many consumer needs. If you want to watch the news, a soap opera or a film, television is fine but watching is a passive process.

The interactive television possibilities offered by CD-I change all this. Viewers can now engage actively with the material which is offered to them. CD-I offers a choice beyond the realm of the on/off switch. With the aid of a simple remote control device, you can use the medium with the same ease as you would use a book. You can browse, select information, scan it, use it, extract from it the data, instruction or entertainment you require, and then leave it.

From entertainment to education, the opportunity to participate in programmes offers greater enjoyment, involvement and retention of information. Now, with CD-I players aimed at the same market as televisions, this opportunity is available to potentially huge audiences.

STORAGE COMPARISONS

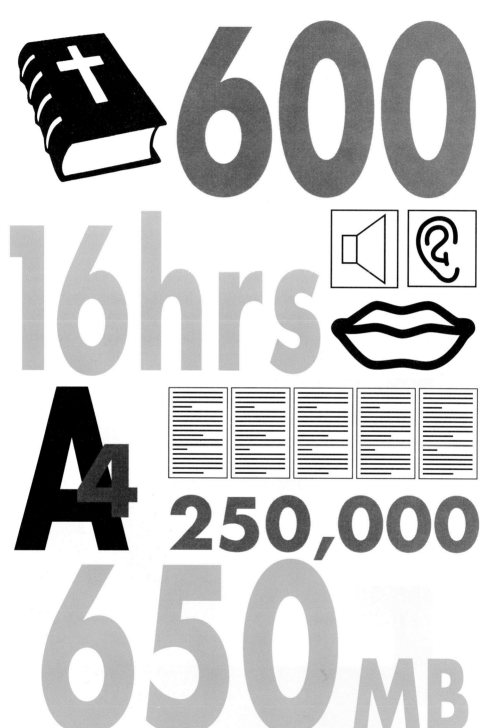

600

16hrs

A4

250,000

650 MB

INTRODUCING *CD-I*

The techniques that have made this all possible explore the possibilities of an ordinary compact disc. You can get 600 copies of the Authorised version of the Holy Bible, or 250,000 typed A4 pages on a compact disc; or, to put it in computer terms, 650 megabytes of data. But CD-I is not just a storage device. It enables you to gain access to information with unparalleled ease and speed, and exploits this capacity to the full to give a multimedia combination of voice, music, text, and moving and static images which act as a vast resource for the audience.

CD-I is portable and browsable, it carries a lot of information in a small space, and you can take from it what you want or you can become totally absorbed in it. But it has other, additional advantages to offer, combining the strengths of media such as music discs, video and ordinary television. Add to this the projected wide availability of CD-I players and the fact that they conform to a fully international standard for which titles are being developed around the world, and you have some idea of the likely power and pervasiveness of the new medium.

MEDIA SYNTAX

In the early days of film, the camera did not move and techniques for cutting between scenes were relatively crude. A language had to be constructed, so that now soap operas routinely play with techniques which would have been incomprehensible to an earlier audience who were unfamiliar with the language of film. The same applies to CD-I: a language and a vocabulary have to be established. Those who make CD-I discs now are a part of this pioneering, language building process, and that is the challenge.

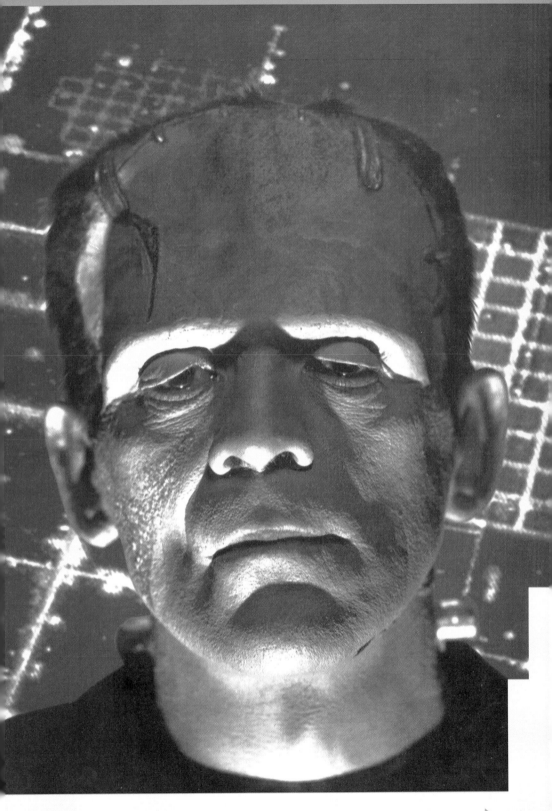

WHAT CAN CD-I DO?

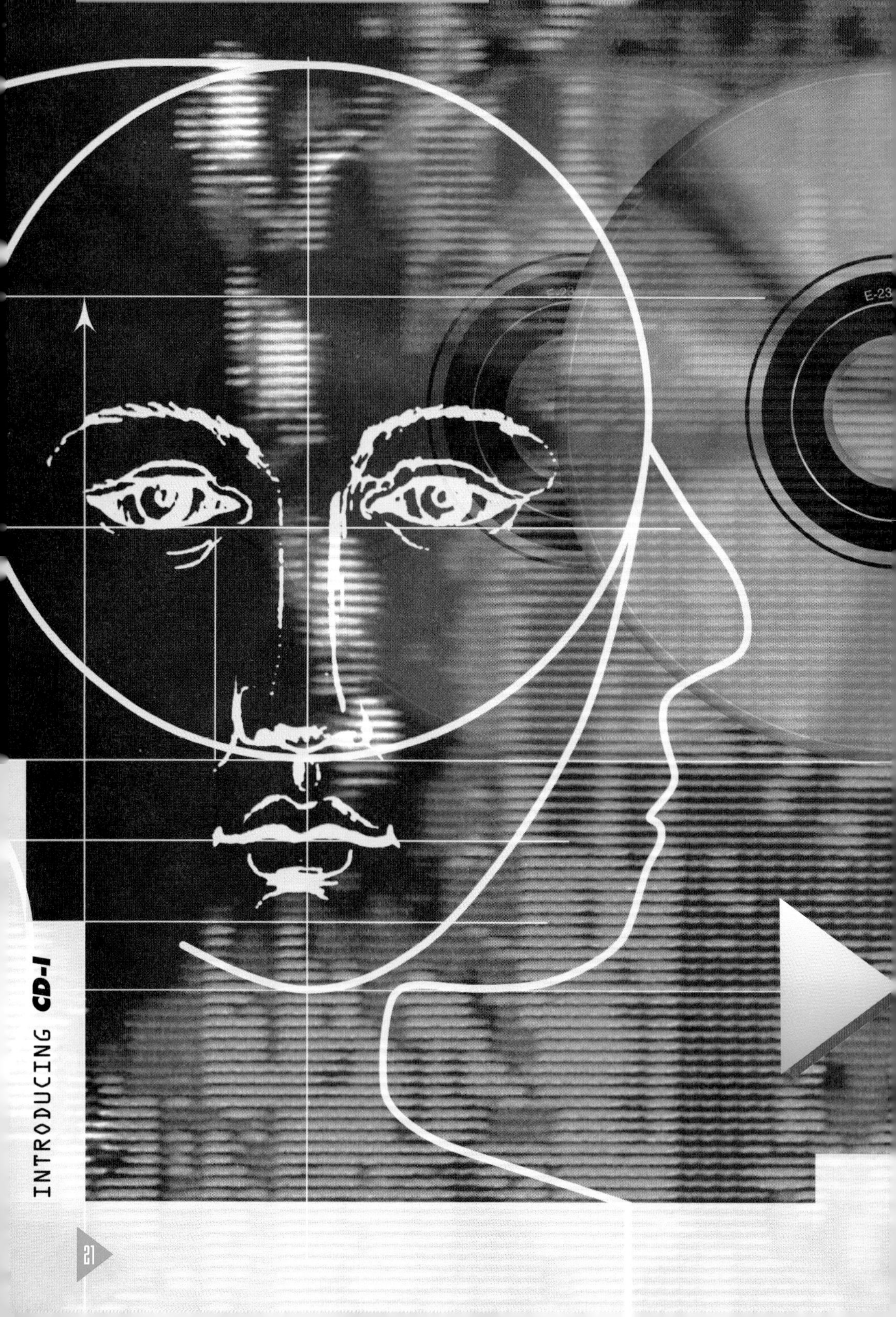

Interactive television is in its infancy. As in the history of other technologies, such as printing, the possibilities are not yet fully apparent. True interactivity is totally new, and requires new ways of thinking. What can be done with it is, for the most part, uncharted, as are the effects upon the perceptions of the people using it. While there is bound to be a market (and a large one) for recycling and adding new life to the products of other media in interactive form, there are outstanding opportunities for people who have the capacity to conceive of truly CD-I ideas - that is, ideas which are truly interactive and multimedia in their approach.

music, movies and plays enhanced with some interactive content

diagnostic reference works (such as animated car repair manuals)

cookery instructions

armchair travel guides to countries, towns, museums, buildings etc

electronic album sleeve notes

critical analyses and guides to books, music and films

simulators (for example, driving lessons)

From car repair manuals to multiple choice

interactive soap operas

drama, from point of sales applications to

in-car navigation system

adventure games, the list of possible

arcade games

applications is endless. Point-of-information,

sports enhanced with record breaking performances & athletic biographies

point-of-sale, reference, training and

children's titles

education, not to mention entertainment, are

home doctors

all areas in which applications may be

language learning

developed. You can use the medium to the

industrial and commercial training material

limit of its interactive multimedia capacity,

historical subjects

or you can use it for less ambitious

games of skill and board games

purposes. You can use the current

personal and public picture libraries

hardware, or you can look at new

catalogues and point-of-sale material

possibilities for remote control devices or

multimedia encyclopaedias and dictionaries

Walkman style players.

personalised fitness and workout instructions

FAMILIAR TECHNOLOGY

You can play CD-I discs on an ordinary
CD-I player which is no bigger than an
ordinary video recorder and connects to the
back of your television set in the same way.

CD-I AND MULTIMEDIA

CD-I players will initially cost only a little more than good quality CD audio players. In addition to playing CD-I discs, they can also be used to play audio CDs and view photographs on Kodak and other photographic CDs. The face which CD-I presents to the audience is one of a reassuringly familiar technology. There is no keyboard and no computer feeling - just a compact disc drive and a television style remote control. The technological leap forward is handled by the player and not the audience. All they have to do is participate in the new experience.

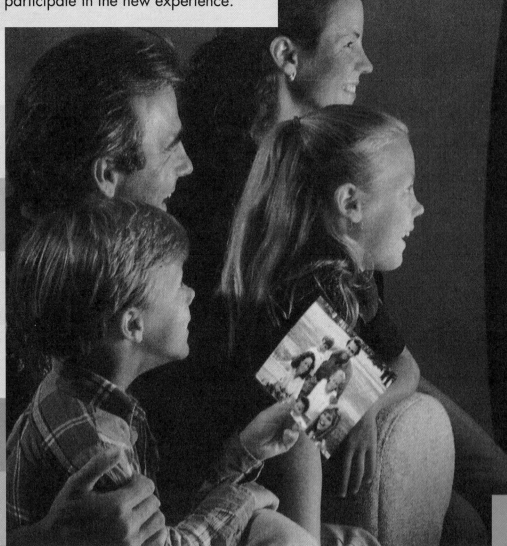

PHOTO CD

2 HOW CD-I WORKS

This chapter looks at CD-I as a medium and the technology behind it. As we have already seen, CD-I appears familiar - like a marriage of other technologies which have found acceptance in homes and other settings. But you need to understand a bit about the technology behind it before you can start to imagine the wealth of possibilities offered by this new medium.

INTRODUCING *CD-I*

Interactivity

Interactivity means that the audience has the chance to decide what it wants to see. Using the remote control to make choices and answer questions, the audience is encouraged to take an active part in deciding just what it wants out of the programme. There is no fixed order to the parts of a programme - choice is the order of the day. Interactivity engages the audience and offers them the benefits of improved involvement, choice and learning.

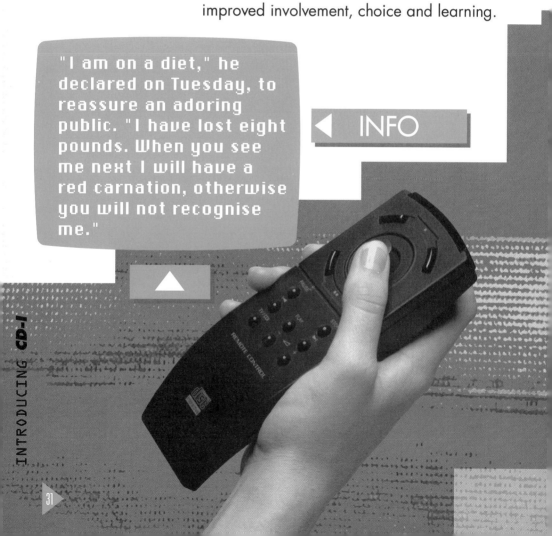

"I am on a diet," he declared on Tuesday, to reassure an adoring public. "I have lost eight pounds. When you see me next I will have a red carnation, otherwise you will not recognise me."

◀ INFO

Revealed: the temptations of Luciano Pavarotti. A trail of marzipan, Gorgonzola cheese, peanuts and champagne leads to the four- poster bed of the world's most hallowed dieter.

PLAY

MULTIMEDIA

Multimedia is the use of a variety of different media in one production. Video pictures, music, animation, text and music are fitted together to create a new type of medium. You might say that films are already multimedia - after all, they also use all these separate media. But once the contents of a film have been put together, they stay in that order - it cannot be changed.

The particular strength of multimedia is less the fact that the different media can be used than that they can be accessed separately. Multimedia is like a library from which you can take an image here, a bit of text there, some video, a snatch of music, a speech, and combine them in a way which fits the context in which they are used. If film welds its elements together once and for all, multimedia combines them, but leaves them available for recombination. The same image, bit of text, snatch of music can be used in a variety of contexts for a number of purposes. A picture of Nelson's column can feature in a guided tour of Trafalgar Square, a survey of English naval history, and an affectionate tribute to pigeons.

Television is available in everyone's home. Add interactivity to multimedia and put them both on television, and the result is something quite new to most people. The interactive multimedia television combination is greater than the sum of its parts.

CD-I is the most recent extension of the concept of interactive multimedia. Previous multimedia technologies have suffered from several drawbacks - they were cumbersome and expensive, they were not widely available, and they were not standardised. Because of these disadvantages, the audience for previous attempts to create interactive multimedia applications has been limited to those who could afford the computers or other specialist equipment needed to make them work. They have been restricted to professional and commercial markets.

CD-I sidesteps these drawbacks to bring high quality multimedia to a mass audience for the first time. The new CD-I players are compact, inexpensive, user friendly and constructed to an international standard. The importance of this last point should not be underrated. The standards jointly established by Philips, Sony and Microware are precisely defined in a document called the Green Book. This is the CD-I developer's bible: all CD-I players and discs must conform to the technical specifications it contains. This ensures that a CD-I disc bought anywhere in the world can be played on any CD-I player anywhere in the world.

NTS

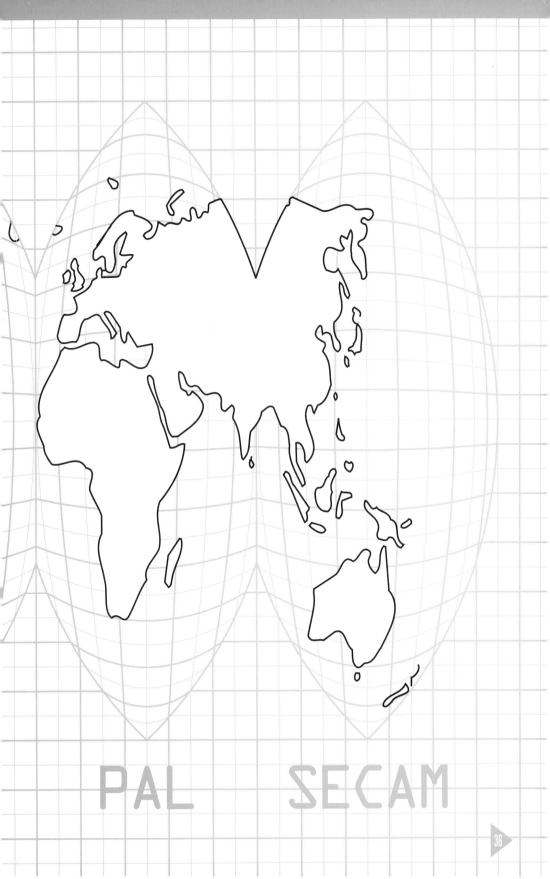

PAL   SECAM

Nearly a quarter of the world's population (1.2 billion people) own televisions, and CD-I is aimed at them. Because CD-I programmes run from a disc and are not broadcast, the number of people watching a programme is not constrained by whether they happen to tune in at the right time. The potential audience for CD-I discs is huge, equalling the figures for the most widely watched programmes. At the same time, CD-I has the potential to make commercial and professional uses of interactive multimedia more widely available. Point-of-sale and point of information programmes will be far easier to commission and install, while even hard-up schools or hospitals will be able to afford players to run educational or diagnostic interactive programs.
CD-I gives interactive multimedia a vast potential audience.

INTRODUCING **CD-I**

A CD-I disc can hold any combination of these materials:

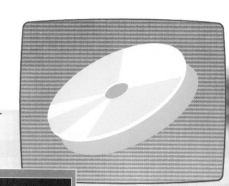

VIDEO PICTURES
Moving colour pictures which take up all or part of the screen

GRAPHICS AND TEXT
From titles to text pages, CD-I offers an enormous storage potential for text and static display of words.

STILL PICTURES
Colour still pictures with a high degree of resolution

SOUND AND MUSIC
CD-I can have all the unrivalled sound quality of CD Audio

INTRODUCING **CD-I**

In making a CD-I disc you can combine these materials to produce precisely the effects you want. Above all, CD-I is versatile. Every function of the disc you can think of can be ideally served by one or other of the media available. For example, a detailed explanation may be best served by a page of text or by a voice over; a mechanical procedure may be illustrated by a sequence of stills, by an animated (cartoon) sequence, or a video clip. CD-I adds interactivity to this wealth of resources. Walking around an art gallery is more satisfying than reading about it. Using an interactive programme comes somewhere between reading about a gallery and walking around it. It offers you a chance to participate in and shape your experience; to ask further questions and pursue lines of enquiry; and to move around as you want, and not as some other person directs you. This involvement increases enjoyment, understanding and retention of information, all of which are essential to education and entertainment. In short, CD-I is a versatile medium which offers both producers and consumers unparalleled availability, ease of access, choice and interactivity.

ANIMATION

Animated pictures are lively and save disc space

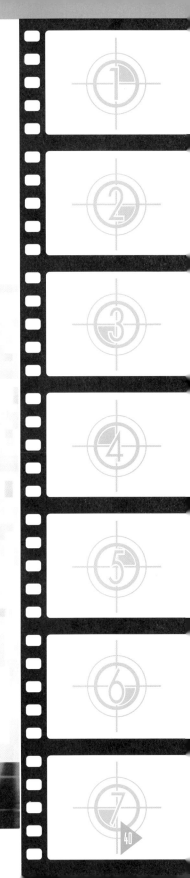

THE IMPORTANCE OF DIGITS

CD-I is a digital medium.

The data stored on the disc, whether it is moving pictures, sound or stills, cartoons or graphics, is stored in digital form. What this means is that the information is coded into a series of noughts and ones. These noughts and ones (represented by pits and bumps on the disc's surface) stand for the sound or picture which is being produced at any instant. This has several advantages over analogue storage methods (such as normal cassette tapes).

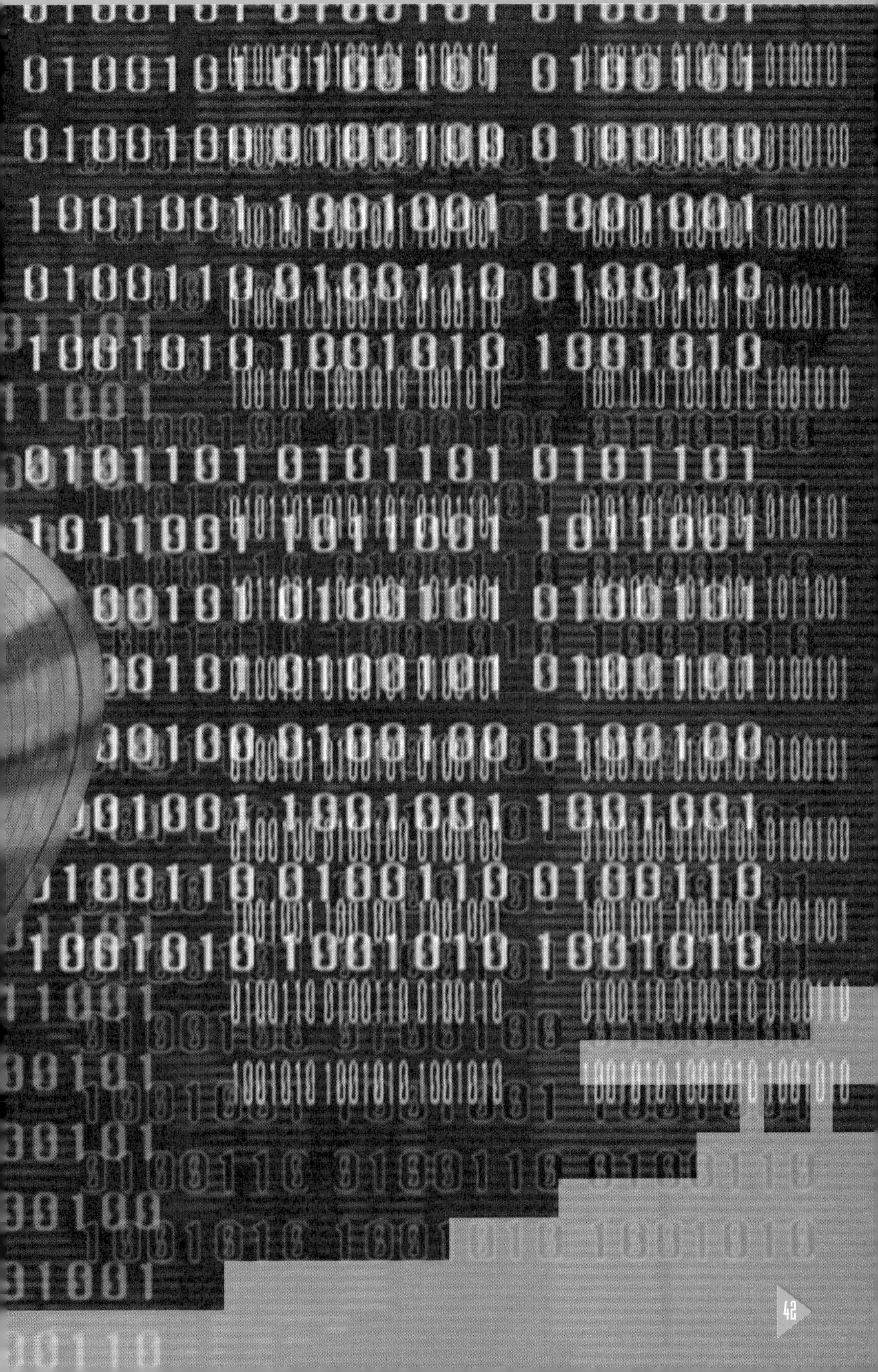

POINTS ABOUT DIGITAL MEDIA

FIRSTLY IT IS MORE RESILIENT.

Digital material does not deteriorate with copying, whereas analogue material does. A picture can be reproduced more accurately with disc pressing than it can be by the analogue copying involved, for example, with VHS video tapes.

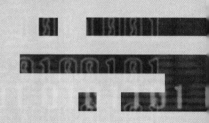

SECONDLY IT IS EASIER TO HANDLE.

Not only cutting from effect to effect, but editing details of pictures and sounds can be carried out with comparatively little expertise on a computer workstation.

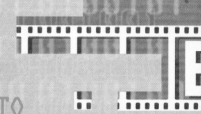

THIRDLY IT IS EASIER TO INTEGRATE DIFFERENT MEDIA TYPES.

Because you can store audio and visual material in the same format, retrieving words, sounds and pictures quickly, and blending them seamlessly together to produce multimedia effects is far easier than it would be with similar materials stored in analogue form.

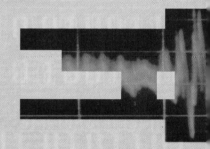

LASTLY, COMPRESSION IS EASIER.

Storing materials as numbers means that certain techniques can be used to compress images and sounds so that you can get more of them on a CD-I disc. For example, the space required to store the information for some moving pictures can be compressed to one tenth of its original size.

INTRODUCING **CD-I**

43

ZAP IT 2
Tales From The Crypt

A single CD-I disc can store any of the following. You probably would not use it in this way because, for example, if you stored 72 minutes of moving pictures, you would not be able to use the highest quality sound. In practice there will always be tradeoffs between the different media. However, it is useful to know the upper limits for each type of material when you make a disc.

UP TO 72 MINUTES MOVING VIDEO PICTURES

UP TO 7 000 FULL COLOUR STILL PICTURES

UP TO 72 MINUTES OR SO OF ANIMATED PICTURES

FROM UP TO 2 HOURS OF HI-FI SOUND TO 19 HOURS OF SPEECH QUALITY SOUND

UP TO 250 000 PAGES OF TEXT

HOW THE MEDIUM AFFECTS THE DESIGN

CD-I, like any medium, has its design constraints. You must use it with understanding in order to exploit its possibilities to the full. When you design for CD-I, there are four main technical factors which you must consider in order to make your design work effectively: disc capacity, memory, data rate and seek time. Remember that beneath its television-like exterior, the CD-I player conceals a powerful computer. The computer is converting digits into sounds and pictures, and responding to the user's interactions. The user does not need to be aware of it, but producers and designers must take these factors into account.

Disc Capacity

The CD-I disc holds 650 megabytes of data. Whatever combination of materials you use, and whatever their quantity and quality, the question must always be asked: Will they all fit on the disc?

Memory

The CD-I player's memory is used to store images and sounds for instant effects such as fading one picture into another. The size of the memory controls what you can do at any one time. For example, you might need to be aware of memory limitations if you were designing complex animation sequences accompanied by audio effects.

INTRODUCING *CD-I*

Data rate

The speed at which data can be read off the disc by the player and turned into pictures or sounds controls how many things you can load or use at one time. For example, you might have around six different language tracks running parallel. You will soon get a feeling for the maximum number of things the player can cope with - but 16 channels for sound and up to 32 for other uses gives you quite a bit of room for manoeuvre.

Seek Time

In a highly interactive programme, the player may have to read data from many different locations on the CD-I disc. A well designed disc will be laid out so that data which are related are grouped close together. The maximum time it takes the player to switch from one part of the disc to another and read an entirely new piece of information is approximately three seconds. Normally it is less than this.

These factors mean that careful planning is the essence of good CD-I design. You want to use the medium to add value for the audience, so you must be sure that what you make is seamless and smooth and does

650 megabytes seems like a lot of storage space to have on a 12 centimetre disc when you compare it with, say, a high density floppy disc for a personal computer of approximately the same size, which holds 1.2 megabytes. But as the previous page showed, its capacity is not infinite. There are limits. Although there may be applications in which you want only full motion video pictures or very high quality hi-fi sound, you are more likely to want to use a mixture of CD-I's various levels of picture and sound quality.

Although the technical details need not concern us here, it is useful to know that there are more than half-a-dozen methods for digitising pictures, and four different levels of sound recording. Each of these different methods or levels takes up more or less space on the disc. The more you want to get onto the disc, the more important it is that you use the level or method which is most economical on disc space and is consistent with your purpose.

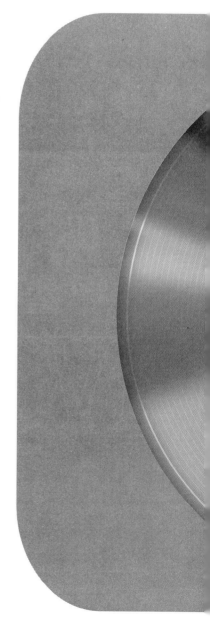

E-234 452 -.LTT822720072RDF

650 MB

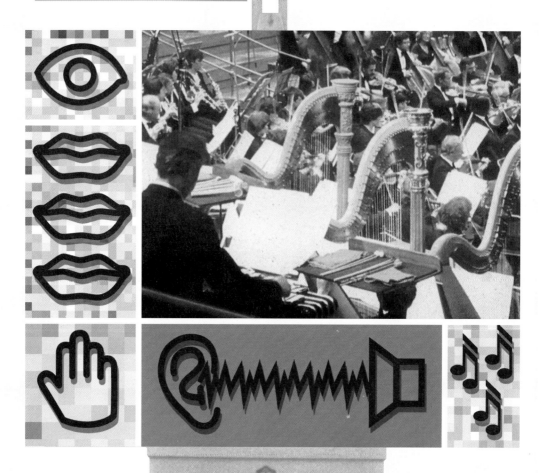

The various ways of digitising pictures suit different types of picture. The method for encoding moving video pictures takes up more space on the disc than that for encoding animated cartoon pictures. This is because photographic images are usually more complicated than drawings, and so need more digits to record their details.

The different sound levels also suit different purposes. If you have a full symphony orchestra and the music it is playing is the focus of attention on the disc, then you would probably use the highest quality hi-fi sound at your disposal. But if you only need a voice-over, you might use speech quality sound, which takes up much less disc space.

INTRODUCING *CD-I*

Filling the disc is like packing a suitcase. You only put in what is absolutely necessary, you make sure that you have the most compact or lightest version of whatever you are taking, and you arrange things so you can find them easily. In practice this often comes down to trading between the various different interests and skills involved in the creation of the disc. Each member of the production team has to justify what they want to the others. But if the CD-I is carefully designed in the first place, then the packing process should be relatively smooth, and it won't be necessary to jump up and down on the suitcase.

The nature of the medium is crucial to the design of CD-I titles. You have to take account of the fact that you have a canvas of a fixed size upon which to work. But in working to CD-I standards you are making a product which has a worldwide market. Everyone involved in the creative process needs to be aware of the resources available to them and the best ways of working together to achieve results. The teamwork and tradeoffs which are necessary for good design, along with good management, are in themselves a stimulus to creativity.

3 CONCEPT AND DESIGN

This chapter gives an introduction to some
of the issues involved in designing CD- I
titles. If you want to know more about CD-I
design, you should read The CD-I Design
Handbook.
Having looked at the reasons for using CD-I,
this chapter considers approaches to design
and outlines the design process before
ending with a list of useful guidelines.

E-234 452 -- LTT182272007RDF

You have seen what CD-I is and what it can do. But how can it work for you? Making a CD-I programme demands a high level of commitment and organisation. Assuming that you have started to think CD-I and have come up with a title (or somebody else has approached you with a likely sounding title), what questions do you need to ask in order to be sure that you are on the right track?

DOES THE TITLE REQUIRE A MULTIMEDIA APPROACH?

It may be that you merely want to use a CD-I disc for a film or music, but since one of the selling points of the medium is its multimedia capacity, it makes sense to use it. Look at the list of possible applications on page 22 - 24 to help you to decide if your title is suitable for multimedia treatment.

DOES THE TITLE REQUIRE INTERACTIVITY?

As with the multimedia approach, you don't have to use interactivity, but it makes sense to do so. Remember the benefits of interactivity - user control, increased involvement and enhanced understanding - it offers in all fields, from education to entertainment.

IS THE TITLE AIMED AT THE SORT OF PEOPLE WHO OWN CD-I PLAYERS?

The answer to this question requires some research. At least initially, the people who buy CD-I players are likely to be the same sort of people who own video recorders and compact disc players. For other more specialist titles, you must consider whether the target audience might easily buy CD-I players (for example, hospitals or factories). In the long term, the projected wide distribution of CD-I players might render this question redundant.

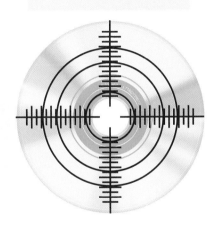

To produce a CD-I programme which uses
its interactive multimedia potential is a
complex task. It may be that a coffee table
book or a television programme is more
appropriate. You have to weigh up the
advantages of each medium in order to
reach your decision.
In many areas, such as education, it may
be desirable to have an accompanying
book. It is worth considering this possibility.

IS IT POSSIBLE TECHNICALLY?

This question is difficult to answer off the
top of your head. You have to consider
whether your material will fit into the
physical space offered by the disc, and
whether the sorts of effect you envision are
indeed possible with CD-I. Having seen
some of the figures on page 18, you are at
least in a position to make a rough guess.
Read The CD-I Handbook to obtain a
clearer and more detailed idea of what is
and isn't possible.

IS IT POSSIBLE FINANCIALLY?

The new state of the art makes it impossible
to give any sort of useful figures. You will
only be able to answer this by doing your
sums using the information about resources
and production given in the next chapter of
this book.

INTRODUCING **CD-I**

Rights for the title, and rights for elements used within the CD-I programme, such as images, music or text, can make up a surprisingly large proportion of total costs. Where rights are likely to be an issue, it is worth looking into their cost and availability early on in planning the project.

IS THE TITLE UNIQUE?

At this stage in the history of CD-I, the title catalogue is small enough for the repetition of titles to be unnecessary and likely to affect sales. For the foreseeable future at least there is enough uncharted territory for everyone to stake a claim of their own.
If you have the right answer to all or most of these questions you are ready to move onto the next stage of the design process.

CORRECT ANSWERS:
YES
YES
YES
YES
YES
YES
YES
AND

YES
YOU
SHOULD
USE
CD-I

Once you have satisfied yourself that CD-I
really is the medium for you, you can start to
look at some issues which have a more direct
impact on the design of your title.
CD-I is interactive television. It is important
to remember both these aspects of the
medium when you design for it.
Interactive means that the idea should
be one in which the likely audience
will be engaged. Television means
that the title must be one which
appeals to a well defined set of
people. There is no room for
vague idealism. The
production of CD-I titles is
no less a precise craft
than the production of
television titles.

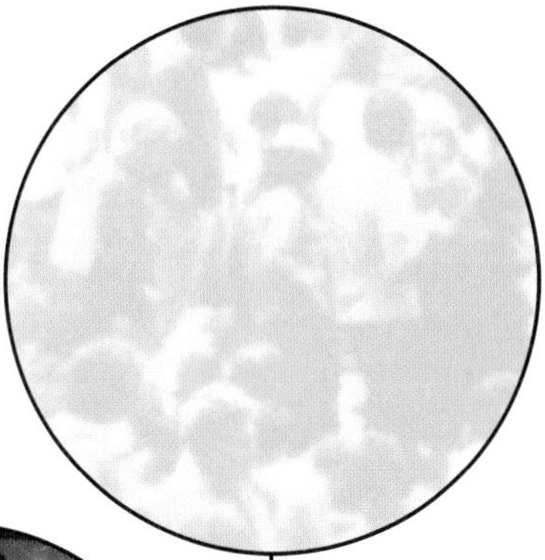

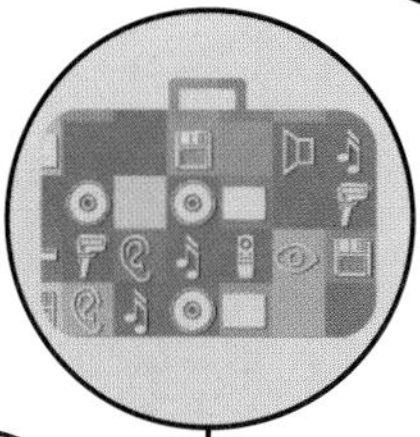

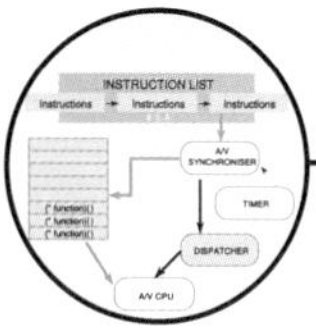

AUDIENCE
PURPOSE
MEDIUM
SPACE
STRUCTURE
INTERFACE
SO

AUDIENCE

More than with any other medium, CD-I addresses its audience very directly. If they are to interact, they have to want to interact, so it is important to have a clear idea of who they are and what they expect.

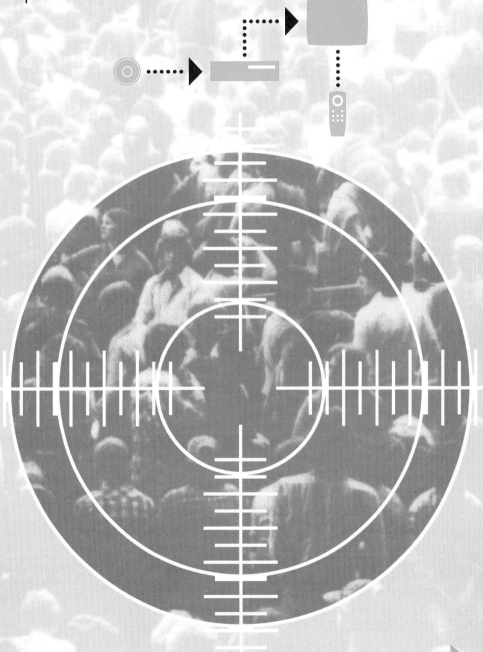

PURPOSE

Connected to the idea of audience is the idea of purpose.
What are you going to do with your audience? For example, do
you want to educate, entertain or train them? (Of course, many titles
will involve a mixture of these intentions.) Each intention may involve
separate design objectives. Education should promote a desire to
explore; entertainment, a complicity; and training, a structured
response.

INTRODUCING **CD-I**

CD-I is a multimedia concept. You have to think how you are going to use the media involved. You may want to use all the possibilities available: video, animation, stills, graphics, music, speech. Or you may only want to use a subset of them. For example, CD-I Ready discs are essentially audio CDs which have the additional feature of electronic sleeve notes - details of the recording and the artists involved. At the other extreme are more elaborate productions involving all the media. You should have a good reason for using each resource: don't just use them because they are there.

Tradeoff

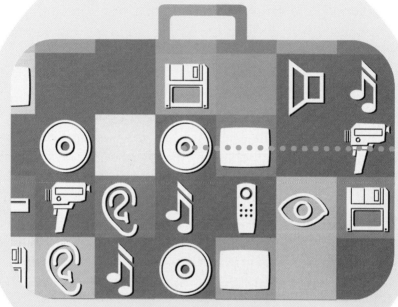

As suitcases go, a CD-I disc is quite a large one, but there are still limits. You may have to leave out the kitchen sink, the foldaway bicycle and the steam iron, but you can still pack everything you need. Look carefully at how much of the most space-consuming media (full screen video, hi-fi sound) you need to use as these can limit the scale of your production. You may have to make calculations like If I have an hour of full screen video, I won't be able to have all those animated sequences I wanted, or If I have the sound of the symphony orchestra in the foreground the whole time, I won't be able to have so many moving pictures. Implicit in this procedure is the business of tradeoffs. Tradeoff is a word which you will hear a lot in CD-I design. Using the space on the disc is a social process - each requirement has to be agreed with everybody else. Tradeoff is a discipline, but, as everybody knows, discipline is good for you.

Working out the structure is the hard bit. You know what you want the product to feel like, but now you have to be more precise. Flowcharts can help to clarify structure, but even for a linear process, working out the ramifications of an idea can be difficult. With a process which involves branching structures this is even more so. However, the problem is not insuperable. A modular approach solves a lot of problems. Once you have started outlining things in more detail (this stage is called developing the treatment), you can use some software applications and authoring packages to test the logic of your design. Before you know it, you have moved to the next stage (storyboarding) and the only thing left to do is assemble the CD-I. Where you choose to take up or leave the process depends upon whether you are designing, producing or publishing CD-I titles.

The approaches outlined in The CD-I Design Handbook enable you to cope with the complexities of multimedia, non-linear design.

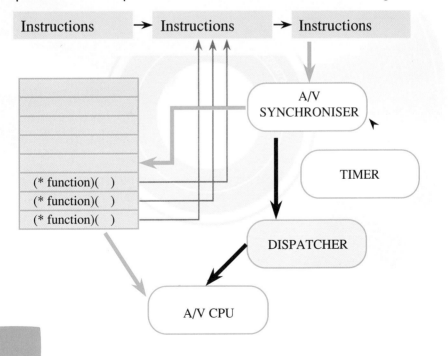

How is the product going to appear to the user? At the software level you have to look at how you are going to handle interactivity. Are you going to use menus or hotspots? Will interactivity be used for navigation, or to control pace or level? Why do you wish to engage your audience or users? At the hardware level, you must look at the equipment available. For example you may choose between touch screens or remote control devices. You can go for a standard device, or you can think about designing your own. There are many other questions you need to ask yourself about how the programme you have designed is going to interact with the audience you are intending to reach.

With a clear idea of your answer to each of these basic questions in mind, you should be in a position to start thinking seriously about the title you have dreamed up. In some senses, thinking of titles is the easy part. As is often the case with any art, it is not having ideas, but putting them into practice which is difficult.

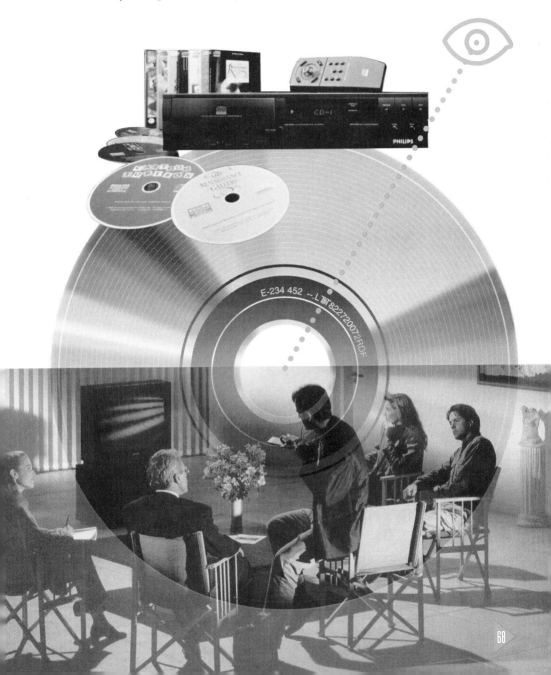

MAKING YOUR IDEA HAPPEN

This section shows the steps in the process of working out an idea. You have a shrewd idea of what you want to do. Now you want to look at details. Scripting a CD-I title is like making a film: you are dealing with a variety of sources and processes. The complication is coordinating and synchronising them.
Here are the stages of the process:

The idea - or spark - behind the whole thing. It can arrive from a number of sources: a client may commission a title. Market analysis can indicate a gap or need in the market. There may be a mass of existing material around from which you can build a title. Or someone may quite simply come up with an idea.

The concept can be anything from an idea on the back of an envelope to a formal proposal - depending on who you are trying to sell it to. For the most part it is an outline which addresses the issues outlined in the next few pages.

As in the film business, the treatment outlines the plot and what you are going to do with it. A treatment for the cinema is easier to create because films have a linear structure; a CD-I treatment usually has to show the branching structure of the material, and is therefore modular.

The design document is a detailed specification for the CD-I disc. Typically, it should contain most of the following:

Overall program flowchart - how the program fits together.

Description - a summary of subject matter, treatment and audience.

Product feasibility assessment - analysis of technical and economic areas showing that the product is possible.

Summary of storage requirements - a list of the materials making up the disc (video, sound, graphics, interactivity etc.), how much disc space they will use, and how they will be fitted onto the disc.

Technical specifications - full design specifications and flowcharts for all levels of the program.

It is at this stage of development that tradeoffs start to become important.

STORYBOARD

An exact visual specification. For animated
sequences, the storyboard is obviously all
important. For video sequences how precise
this is depends upon the sort of people
creating the visuals. Hitchcock storyboarded
everything and stuck to his storyboard, but
Robert Altman makes it up as he goes along.
Screen layouts, audio scripts and other
working specifications. These are the
materials from which the various parts of the
production will be made - the words,
pictures and graphics which will end up
recorded in digital form on the disc.

In addition to these, you will have all the
usual management documents to consider,
such as an implementation plan (who does
what, when and where), a validation plan
(including details of testing and prototyping),
and a detailed budget.

Without wandering into the realm of taste or aesthetics, it is possible to lay down certain ground rules. Given that the language of CD-I is emerging, these rules may change or be challenged.

START SIMPLE

Keep your first productions simple. Use the first titles to acquire the skills which will enable you to carry through more complicated ideas later on.

INTRODUCING *CD-I*

DON'T BE TOO CLEVER

CD-I is a complex medium with lots of potential. However, there is no need to put it through all its paces on every outing. While this may - or may not - impress other designers of interactive CDs, it is not necessary and may even be confusing for the audience. Economy of means applies as much to the design of CD-I titles as to any other type of design. A simple structure and an easy-to-understand interface will hold the attention of an audience far better than one which is baroque and labyrinthine.

MAKE IT ATTRACTIVE

This sounds obvious, but it is worth remembering that CD-I is intended primarily as a consumer medium. Even in training and less commercial applications, you still need to grab the attention of the audience and keep it. Software games designers call this quality *hookability*, and it is for CD-Is what *I couldn't put it down* is for novels.

MAKE IT LAST

A CD-I programme should be more like an LP which you listen to lots of times than a film which you may only look at once or twice. For this reason, avoid effects which are likely to become irritating when you have encountered them more than once. This quality is called lastability, and involves the skillful use of levels of detail and difficulty to keep the interest of the audience, as well as demanding simple and unfussy design.

MAKE IT INTERACTIVE

Make it interactive if that is what you want (you could just use the CD-I disc as a convenient method of packaging music or films). Interactivity is the feature of CD-I which adds value to the product. It engages the audience and enhances hookability and lastability.

INTRODUCING **CD-I**

CREATE A CONSISTENT REALITY

The world the audience enters when it uses the CD-I player should be consistent and credible. In this respect, the world of computer games has something to teach the makers of applications which are less obviously entertainment. The look you create for any title should go right through the product, from menu screens to the packaging. Whatever type of CD-I you are making, coherence and consistency make the product identifiable and easy to use, and hold the attention of the audience.

KEEP LOOKING

The only way to get the feel of the CD-I you are building is to take frequent looks at it. The authoring systems used to put the CD-I title together make it possible to run the programme and see how it works. You can also cut one-off trial discs known as WORM (Write Once Read Many) discs. These are the best way of spotting any awkwardnesses in the programme. For example: are the pauses between items too long? does the music sound right with the pictures? does a transition between two images produce some unforeseen effect? does it look and feel like you want it to look and feel?

The multimedia nature of CD-I means that a large number of different talents are involved in the creation of a title. Each of the people involved in the process, from writers to programmers has to have an understanding of what the rest of the team do. If the writer knows what the programmer does then he or she can write in a way which is easy to program. If the programmer knows what the writer does, he or she can make programs which are appropriate to, or even facilitate the writing process.

Tradeoffs are the essence of the design process. The object of tradeoffs is to use the highest appropriate quality of digital storage for each element of the design in order to make the maximum amount of space available. Tradeoffs are a product of teamwork, with each person claiming what they require and conceding what they do not in order to reach a balanced solution.

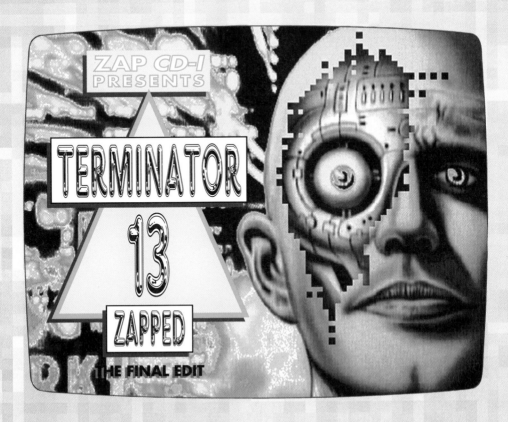

DESIGN FOR SEQUELS

In making a CD-I title, you are also inventing a vocabulary of tricks and processes. It is pointless to reinvent this vocabulary every time. If, for example, you have developed some neat navigational devices, you can use them again in other titles. This has two advantages: it gets the maximum use out of the work you have done; and it gives the audience familiar landmarks which make them feel comfortable and identify your products.

MAKE UP NEW RULES

CD-I is a new medium. There are many technical and formal possibilities to be explored. So make up new rules.

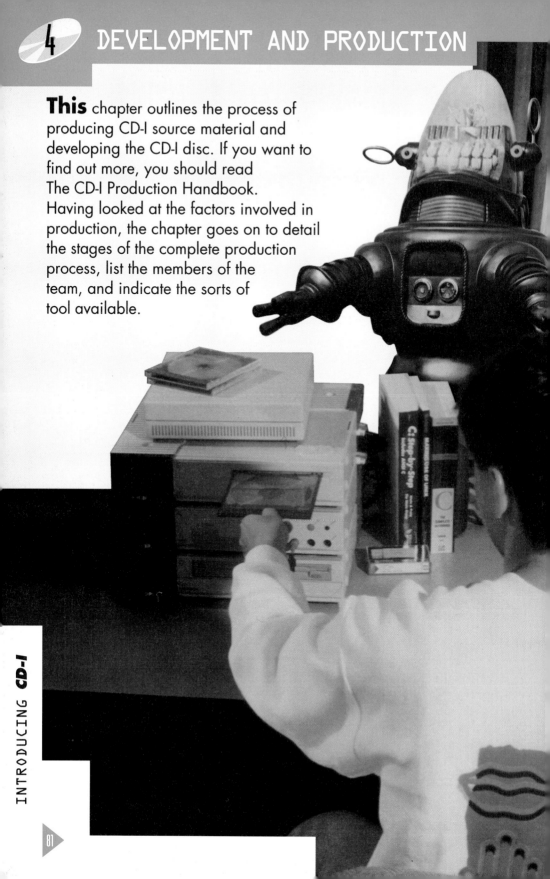

This chapter outlines the process of producing CD-I source material and developing the CD-I disc. If you want to find out more, you should read The CD-I Production Handbook. Having looked at the factors involved in production, the chapter goes on to detail the stages of the complete production process, list the members of the team, and indicate the sorts of tool available.

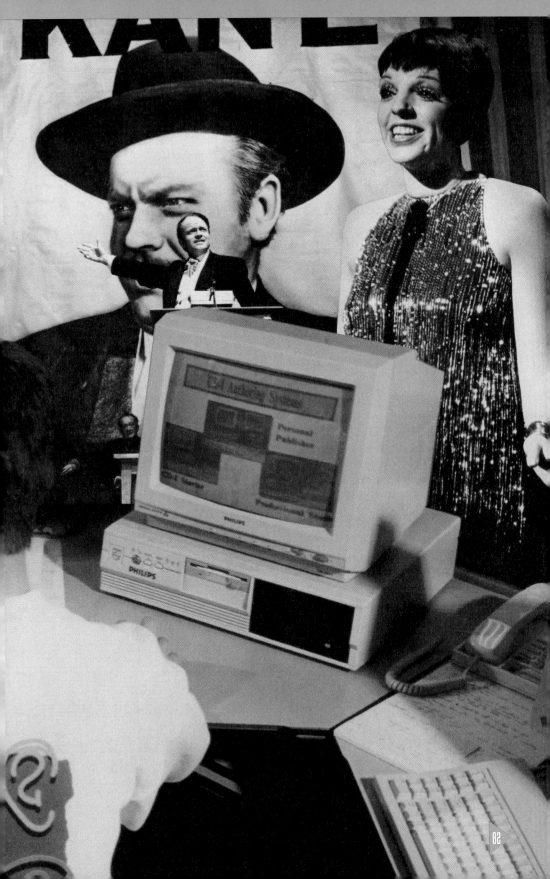

APPROACHES

As we have already seen, multimedia production is a complex process. All the resources required, whatever the medium, have to end up in the same format - that is, as digital information suitable for the CD-I disc. These resources then have to be organised and manipulated into a coherent product. The end of the process, which must always be kept in mind, is the disc which will slot into a CD- I player and serve a well defined purpose.

The production process divides into two sorts of activity:

1. **Production of source materials.**

2. **Production of the control program and disc building.**

Another way of looking at it is that the control program is the framework and that the materials have to be hung upon this frame. Production of source materials extends from the initial conception of the idea for the CD-I title, through storyboarding to such activities as recording sound and video sequences, and making animations and graphics. This process might typically involve writers, video producers, audio producers, animators and graphic artists.

Software production is the process of getting all these resources into digital form suitable for CD-I, and integrating them into the linked structure demanded by the concept for the disc and the user's interaction. This process uses the skills of software engineers and programmers.

Once you have done as much to create and shape the materials as you can, you must start to weld them together. This process is known as authoring, although bolting together might be a more accurate term. The nuts and bolts are bits of software. The main instruments used in this process are authoring platforms and software libraries. These are machines and software for assembling all your materials into the structure you have decided upon.

An authoring platform can be anything from a simple standalone workstation running some fairly basic software, to software running on a sophisticated networked system. They enable you to make the links between different parts of the programme and to set up menus and modes of interaction. They include editing facilities, so you can chop your materials up into the right lengths for use.

They also enable you to view the results of the editing and stitching together process, so you can make sure that you are achieving the desired effects. Some even include graphics packages, so you can design simple menu layouts and information screens.

The platform you decide to use depends upon the complexity of your product, the resources at your disposal, and the production task you are carrying out. If you cannot carry out authoring processes in-house, then you may have to go to a studio and have it done for you. In either case, some knowledge of the production process is an asset.

AUTHORING PLATFORMS

At the most basic level, still images and sound sequences can be manipulated using a simple authoring platform. This can be a straightforward and very effective way of putting together slide and music presentations, but still offers all the benefits of interactivity. For example, a current basic authoring package contains graphics facilities and a range of clip art which enable you to create attractive graphics for title sequences, text pages and menus. Using already existing resources and limited studio facilities, it is quite possible for a small team to produce, for example, company promotional material or point-of-sale programmes.

The simplest platforms have another use - they can be invaluable at an early stage of development for testing and prototyping designs. Although you may have got your design and your logic right on paper, it is not until you put it together that you can make sure it really makes sense from the user's point-of-view.

Slightly more sophisticated platforms are those which allow the manipulation of moving images and the use of subtler editing effects. Typically these run on a personal computer or a standalone workstation, and offer a wider range of editing facilities, and a more powerful graphics package.

INTRODUCING **CD-I**

LIBRARIES

So far we have been talking about authoring platforms as software packages which run on a variety of hardware including dedicated workstations, personal computers and networked workstations.
On a more technical level there are so-called software libraries. These are bits of software which are designed to achieve the effects which together make up the syntax of CD-I programmes. A typical example would be a piece of software which makes one image fade into another. These are the inherited wisdom of CD-I. These pieces of software are collected into libraries, and are used by programmers to create CD-I titles. Obviously they offer greater flexibility and more opportunities for fine-tuning, but this gain must be set against the fact that you need more advanced programming skills to use them.
So...
In the creation of a title you may use any of these approaches. The technology of CD-I is progressing so fast that the simpler packages are rapidly becoming able to do things which only the more sophisticated ones formerly did. And the range of authoring possibilities is expanding all the time.

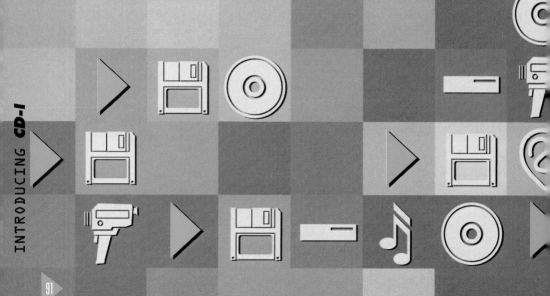

DISC BUILDING

For disc building - that is assembling all the video and audio materials through emulation - making the program run from the mass of data on a hard disc as it would if it were held on a CD-I disc authoring platforms and software libraries are used. When you reach the limits of your competence, you can call in the expertise of a commercial production house to help you. They can either put the whole thing together for you, or simply help you with the finishing touches. At this point you may choose to burn a WORM (Write Once Read Many) disc to test that the interactivity works properly.

The end of the process is called mastering. This involves transferring the data from the hard disc to a tape. The tape then goes to a studio where it is made into the mould from which copies of the disc will be pressed. From there it is a short step to the mass production and distribution of your title.

E-234 452 --.LTT82272007?RDF

E-234 452 --.LTT822720072PDF

E-234 452 --.LTT822720012

The people involved in the process are one of the main resources involved in production. Although a couple of people can put together a simple music and slide presentation on a Starter Kit in a day, larger projects involve much greater resources of people and expertise

Running a larger CD-I project successfully is first and foremost a matter of teamwork. CD-I is multidisciplinary; to make it truly multimedia, the individual disciplines have to work together, so it is important that the individual team members should work together too. Here (in alphabetical order) are some of the people you might need. Obviously you may or may not have all of these - depending upon the nature and scale of the production. Also some team members may have more than one function - and any of them (or all of them) might also be an interactive designer. The precise size and composition of the team will have been identified at the design stage of title development.

ACCOUNTANTS
Coordinate the project budget.

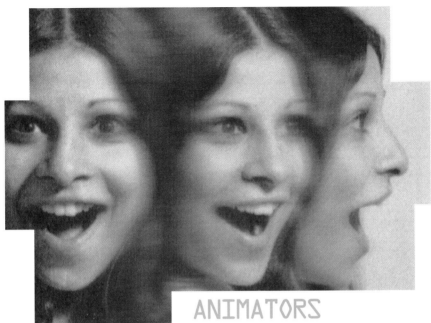

ANIMATORS

Animation is a useful way of entertaining and conveying information which is particularly suited to CD-I and economical with disc space.

ART
DIRECTORS

Control the look of the title.

AUDIO DESIGNERS/ENGINEERS

Record and manipulate the sound elements
and make new ones.

GRAPHIC DESIGNERS

Design images, screens, menus, titles
and text layouts.

INTERACTIVE DESIGNERS

Are specialists in the design of interactive
material. They may be responsible for overall
scripting and for the look and feel of the title.

INTRODUCING *CD-I*

97

PRODUCERS

The producer may have overall control of the project. In addition, you may have separate producers looking after different aspects of the CD-I production - for example: video sequences, music, animation.

PROGRAMMERS

Construct interactivity and software effects.

PROJECT MANAGERS

Manage the day to day running of the project
and make sure that deadlines get hit.

SCRIPT WRITERS

Write anything from the outline of the title
(contained in the treatment) to the words
used in particular contexts.

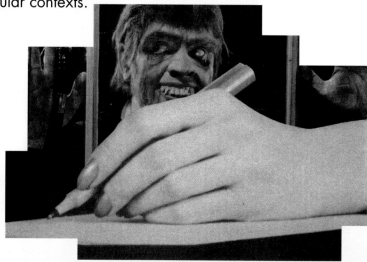

SOFTWARE DESIGNERS

Design the framework for the whole
program (the control program), and are
responsible for disc building.

SUBJECT MATTER EXPERTS

Provide information relevant to the title you are
developing.

TECHNICAL CONSULTANTS

Provide, for example, advice and guidance in
making interactive programs. Help the
producer to co-ordinate the whole enterprise.

DECIDING FACTORS

The level at which you enter the CD-I
development process is determined by:
the scope of the project
the resources available
For a large scale consumer programme, the
production process compares with
production in other media.

ZAP IT 2
Tales From The Crypt
18

£$

INTRODUCING **CD-I**

THE WHOLE SEQUENCE

Although CD-I production is still in its infancy, a normal production sequence is likely to move through the stages described on the next few pages. The stages and processes described are only suggestions. The process will vary according to the size and scope of the project and whether or not there is an external client.

E-234 452 – LTT822720072RDE

CONCEPT

The concept stage covers all activities before a producer is found for the title.

BRIEF

A description given to one or more producers. Its function is a tender put out to likely contractors.

DESIGN PROPOSAL

Producers return design proposals to the client, in which their concept for the design is outlined along with the likely costs.

AGREEMENT

The client and the producer sign an agreement to proceed with the treatment.

TREATMENT

The treatment is described on page 71. It is a synopsis of the 'plot' of the CD-I.

CONTRACT

The contract is signed on the basis of the treatment. It is associated with the following three documents/specifications.

TEAM

The details of the key people working on the project.

BUDGET

Estimates of how much the project is going to cost. Could be (for example) fixed price or time and materials.

SCHEDULE

Deadlines for the various stages of the project.

DESIGN

At this stage all design and planning should be worked out to a high level of detail, to enable programmers, developers and audio/video producers to create interlocking multimedia sources. This is the stage at which the thorough planning essential to CD-I production takes place.

PROJECT PLANNING

Details of how the project is to be managed and organised.

ANALYSIS

Breaking the outline of the 'plot' contained in the treatment into modules. This can be done using techniques such as flowcharting. This involves starting at the concept, breaking it down into components, examining each component and breaking that down again if necessary. The end product of the process is the specification.

SPECIFICATION

A detailed and precise description of every aspect of the title. This includes flowcharts, descriptions of the subject matter, storyboards, full technical specifications, a summary of material requirements and details of every aspect of the product up to and including packaging. This is a working description from which all the people involved should be able to create the separate bits which go to make up the CD-I. It may also include a prototyped module.

DEVELOPMENT

This stage consists of creating and assembling the materials which make up the contents of the disc.

PROJECT MANAGEMENT

Running the project on a day to day basis.

MATERIAL DEVELOPMENT

Creating and obtaining source materials (including ones from external sources) and putting them into CD-I digital format.

SOFTWARE TOOL DEVELOPMENT

Making tools which perform certain functions within the program.

PROGRAMMING

Writing the code for the control program.

DISC BUILDING

Hanging the various material (pictures, words, music etc) on the frame of the control program.

TESTING AND EMULATION

Testing the logic and the look of the program.

VALIDATION

Making sure that the entire program(me) works as it is intended to do, and is ready to be cut onto an optical disc.

PRODUCTION

This is the stage which sees the completed title leave the studio as a master tape, pass through the manufacturing process and appear as a CD-I title in the shops.

MASTERING

The title is transferred from the hard disc of the computer where it has been developed via tape, to become the mould for pressing a CD-I disc. For small numbers of copies it may be preferable to cut WORM (Write Once Read Many) discs.

REPLICATION

Multiple copies of the disc are made from the master.

PACKAGING

Packing the title ready for distribution.

DISTRIBUTION

The title appears at the place where it will be used - at the point-of-sale, in schools, shops etc.

THE BRITISH GOLF MUSEUM

Scotland is the traditional home of golf - the earliest reference to the game was in 1457, when it was banned along with football for keeping King James II's subjects from their archery practice. Scotland is also the home of the British Golf Museum. Opened in 1990, it is situated beside the famous Old Course at St Andrews.

The history of golf and the people who play it is longer and more interesting than most people suspect. Making it come alive is one of the aims of the British Golf Museum. That process involves taking history out of the history books and presenting it in a lively and interesting fashion which appeals to a wide spectrum of people - the sort of people who visit the museum. They have to be entertained and involved. Along with historical exhibits and memorabilia there are also displays of golfing fashions, photographs and a video theatre. But the main attraction for many are the eleven visitor activated touch-screens which allow the viewer to select what they want to hear and see of past golfing glories - places, characters, championships, fashions and equipment.

When the three parties involved in the equipping and programming of the touch screens saw how interested visitors were in the content and style of interactive TV presentation, it seemed entirely logical to gather together the software from the eleven touch screen systems for publishing on a single CD-I disc which became known as Great British Golf.

At the suggestion of Philips, Peter Lewis, the Museum Director, developed a script which used some of the multimedia possibilities of CD-I, and also the ability of CD-I to allow users to find their own preferred path through the programme.

Ted Toms of APS thought that CD-I could add even more value to the title than had been realised. After all, golf is a game, so why not include a game of 'Old Time' golf. By combining information with fun and learning with entertainment the history of golf could be brought alive to a wide audience. The title could be transformed from an exciting museum display into a disc which could be sold to a wide public.

APS set about giving the disc a broader appeal. The history was still there, but added to the package were a Golf trivia quiz and a game on the St Andrews golf course between selected historical characters.

THE CONCEPT

By the time the idea for Great British Golf had got to the concept stage, it had already evolved some way from its starting point. From being a straightforward multimedia history presentation, it had become an exciting piece of 'edutainment'.

Apart from adding the trivia quiz and the golf game to the title, APS and the Philips team came up with some strong ideas for the look and feel. Golf is a game which depends upon the particular. A certain course, the choice of club, unpredictable weather conditions and individual players all conspire together to ensure that no game resembles any other. Standard computer graphics and animation have a levelling quality which is not really in tune with golf's rugged individualism. So it was decided to use graphics and animation generated by hand by a graphic artist.

The concept, then, was of a piece of edutainment which would use all the excitement of CD-I while preserving the eccentric and curious nature of the game of golf.

Because the idea was already well developed by concept stage, a script existed and the title had been accepted by Philips as worth developing, a detailed treatment was not necessary. In more normal circumstances a treatment specifying the structure, description, feasibility, storage requirements and implementation plan would have been produced. This treatment would have been the basis upon which a decision to proceed with the title or not would have been based.

At this stage, too, a demonstration or prototype would normally have been produced. Certainly, if you were trying to sell the idea to a publisher, this would be an essential item. A typical prototype might last for several minutes and demonstrate the 'look and feel' of the title and the way in which the interactivity operates.

Instead of this, Great British Golf went straight from concept to a detailed technical specification. If you are thinking of making a CD-I, however, you should have ready responses to all these issues. CD-I is a precise art, and knowing what you are doing from the start is important in making it possible.

This was the blueprint for the title, the working brief.

Once a script and a storyboard had been produced, discussions took place between the main people concerned. APS were to be responsible for creating the materials (assets) involved in the production, including the script and artwork. Philips were to be responsible for converting the assets into digital format, doing any last minute editing, and bolting the bits together to make the finished CD-I title.

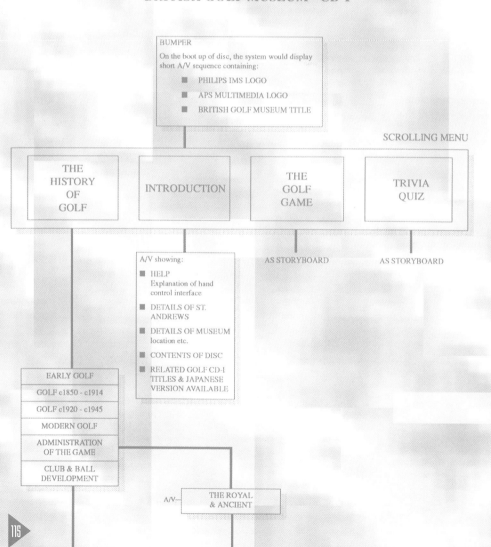

Philips line producer Tamsin Willcocks was responsible for coordinating the storyboard and script into a form which would make sense both to producers and to software engineers. To do this, she used HyperCard stacks.

Each card contained details of visuals, script, sound, interactivity and timing. They could be printed and circulated. They also had the advantage that larger amounts of text could be held on each card and consulted by looking at the stack on a Macintosh. These could be used at all stages of creating and producing assets.
From the detailed script and storyboard, Richard Soppelsa and the software team extracted a list of interactive points and the use of picture planes as a basis for the writing of the code for the title. This was contained in a detailed software specification.

Meanwhile, Tamsin Willcocks analysed the script and drew up an asset list. This was a list of all the bits of audio and video material which the production would require. It would be her responsibility to organise and co-ordinate the process of creating all these bits and pieces and ensure their prompt delivery to the software team for cementing together into the title.

She also drew up a complete list of all the elements of every module of the programme.

Although this is not the only way of doing things, this stage is vitally important in the making of a CD-I title. Because of the close interdependence of all parts of a CD-I programme, any change which is made later on in the production process tends to have a ripple effect. For example, a different image type might require a change in sound quality as well as alterations to software, which might, in turn, affect other parts of the programme. So it is important to try to get things right as far as possible at this early stage.

DEVELOPING ASSETS

If the rest of the production process sounds a bit like software development, this is the bit that comes closest to other types of creative work like making television.

Tamsin Willcocks had already devised a convention for naming the audio and video materials which would allow for multiple versions and different states of each asset. Now it was necessary to make them.

An actor was brought in to read the script. There were many small snatches of audio which had to be digitally recorded and then carefully labelled.

At APS, a freelance artist was brought in to produce the storyboard. He got on with researching the topic and interpreting the script into a series of key pictures. As each piece of material was finished, it was sent off to the studios at Philips Interactive Media.

At Philips, David Furlow's team in the studio scanned images and digitally recorded sound, getting everything into a form in which it could be put on a CD-I disc.

But even at this stage, design decisions had to be made. When the animators started filling in the action, in keeping with the initial design decision, they worked in the traditional way. That is, each cel or frame was drawn then coloured by hand. The images were then scanned and stored on a computer as digital information. Later, it was discovered that hand coloured images used a lot of computer storage space, so the decision was taken to scan only the line drawings for the animation, then colour them cel by cel on the computer. This avoided the uncertainties of hand colour that cost so much storage space.

Another design decision dictated by the capacity of the CD-I player was using partial screen motion (that is a moving picture taking up only part of the screen).

One important consideration was that each asset should be as complete as possible. That is, pictures should have been sized, film edited and sound and music made to last the right length of time for the slot in the programme they were to fit into. This was done using a variety of tools. For example, the cels for the animated sequences were coloured on a Macintosh computer using a paint package. Sound was recorded on digital audio tape and edited on a Macintosh. The opening image (a long horizontal collage) was scanned in sections on a flat bed scanner.

Once each asset had been completed, whether a piece of graphics, an animated sequence, a piece of moving video or a sound sequence, it was carefully labelled and put on the computer network at Philips, from where the software team could access it and start to weld it into the overall structure.

The programming team at Philips were now able to access the assets from the computer network and begin to bolt them together using software engines and other devices. Taking pieces of standardised software (such as the instructions which fade one image into another) from a so called library, and following the instructions worked out by Richard Soppelsa, the programming team slowly changed a set of assets into a fully interactive CD-I title.

Of course this is not the only way of going about putting assets together. Great British Golf was a production which was ambitious in scale and design. Not everyone has, or wants, a team of software engineers and C programmers. In such cases, an authoring package can be used to edit the assets together on a computer or a CD-I emulator. Authoring packages are continuously improving, and allowing non-programmers to achieve sophisticated CD-I effects without too much effort.

Throughout the authoring process, the bits of the programme being developed are run on an emulator. This is simply another name for a CD-I player which runs the programme from its hard disc of a computer instead of from a CD-I disc.

Emulating or testing is important for all sorts of reasons. Apart from the obvious requirement of making sure that everything works as it should in a purely functional sense (does the interactivity work? does the program structure work? and so on) this is also a chance to check the look and feel of the title. It is like looking at the rushes of a film: it is really the only way to judge whether the production is working as intended. What looks good as a piece of artwork in isolation may perhaps lack something when it is incorporated into the body of the title. For example, the pictures of the Old Course, while looking very pleasing and working well in themselves, seemed uncannily silent in their new multi media context. At this point the design team decided that some ambient sound was required. In keeping with the atmosphere of the Old Course they wanted seashore sounds.

The late incorporation of seashore sounds also demonstrates the importance of trying to get everything right at the design stage. The re-recording with ambient sound was expensive but necessary. Because the Great British Golf title was in some ways a pathfinding title it was decided that the extra expenditure could be born. In another situation with a tighter budget, another decision could have been made.

When the whole title had been assembled, an even more demanding form of testing took place. The contents of the computer hard disc were transferred to an optical CD using WORM (Write Once Read Many) technology.

This is the most exacting sort of test, since it exactly reproduces the way in which the final disc will play. Read times (the time it takes to read information from the disc and present it on screen) and interactivity are more precisely simulated than they can be on an ordinary emulator.

Stringent quality controls were carried out at this stage. Tamsin Willcocks drew up a questionnaire which was designed to make sure users asked all the right questions. A number of golf clubs were designated as beta test sites, which meant that they received a player and the disc free in return for feedback about their reactions. Their reactions were the basis of the last few changes to be made to the programme before a master copy was made.

```
!
! golf.m
!
! SCCS ID: @(#)golf.m   1.9   9/17/91
!
! Modified : AT, 2 Aug 91 - include 'cdi_bpsys' in disc image
!            AT, 8 Aug 91 - include 'clean_disc.grn' in disc image
!            AT, 12 Aug 91 - application name is 'cdi_great_golf'
!            AT, 23 Aug 91 - double loader
!            AT, 27 Aug 91 - 'clever' loader - first loader is the main Golf
!                            program
!            AT, 17 Sept 91
!

define album "Golf" publisher "IMS" preparer "Allan, Ken, Steve & Alan"

volume "Golf" in "IMAGE

message from "/e

copyright file C
abstract file Ab
biblio file Bibl

application file

yellow file load

yellow file cdi_

green file clean

green file Green
green file game_
green file trivi

yellow file garb

!yellow file att
!yellow file bac
!yellow file bui
!yellow file cmp
!yellow file code
!yellow file copy      from "/
!yellow file da        from "/home/u1/bin.os9/CMDS/da"
!yellow file date      from "/home/u1/bin.os9/CMDS/date"
!yellow file dcheck    from "/home/u1/bin.os9/CMDS/dcheck"
!yellow file debug     from "/home/u1/bin.os9/CMDS/debug"
!yellow file deiniz    from "/home/u1/bin.os9/CMDS/deiniz"
!yellow file del       from "/home/u1/bin.os9/CMDS/del"
```

When everyone was happy that the title was as good as it could be, the master copy (disc image) was sent off to the factory and a master was made. From this master further copies of the title were made.

At this stage, the covers for the disc were printed and put into the jewel case. The packaged title was then sent to shops and stores for distribution in the conventional way.

The team

This seems a good point at which to look at some of the people involved in the project. Because these are pioneering days in the development of CD-I, the roles taken by people are not as clear cut as they might be in a more developed industry. Above all the most important thing was team work: from regular monthly meetings at which problems were talked out and tradeoffs made, to the countless lesser contacts at which problems and knowledge were shared. Here are a few of the key people.

Peter Lewis

As Director of the British Golf Museum Peter Lewis represented the holders of the copyright on many of the materials used in making the title. This simplified the problem of copyright, since most materials came from one place.

Peter was also subject expert for the history section of the disc, being the person who best knew what some of the more exotic technical terms meant.

Ted Toms

Ted Toms of APS was the Producer of the project. He was responsible for the purely creative side of the project - sourcing and creating artwork, and developing the look and feel. It was Ted's decision to use hand-done in preference to computer generated artwork. On this project Ted did not get too involved with the technical side of production - that was left to Philips.

INTRODUCING *CD-I*

Alan Macnaught

Alan Macnaught of Philips Interactive Media was the Executive Producer. This is essentially the business management and administrative role, although that does not mean that he had no input on the creative side. However it does mean that he was involved in approving expenditure and making sure that what was being made was a product which had more than just a local application.

David Furlow

Notable for the wide extent of his interactive multimedia expertise, David Furlow combines design skills with a very extensive technical knowledge of the possibilities and limitations of technical production. When material arrived from Ted Toms at APS, it was the responsibility of David Furlow's team to convert it all into digital form and to do any final editing on screen that could not be done by APS. He was also responsible for recording the soundtrack. By straddling the gap which often divides creative and technical areas, David's team were key to the whole operation.

Tamsin Willcocks

As line producer, Tamsin Willcocks' job was to make sure that all the wild creative energy that was floating around was firmly pinned down into a list of assets, each named and put on the computer where it could be found by whoever needed it. Quality was also part of her remit. Nothing could be used in the title which had not been approved and labelled by Tamsin.

Richard Soppelsa

The software manager. From the initial plan, Richard Soppelsa's team designed and wrote the interactive programme. The task was not as straightforward as ordinary computer programming, however. What was involved was quality of image and sound and smoothness of effect as much as the execution of lines of code, and this is something which is harder to nail down.

Great British Golf demonstrates the capacity of CD-I simultaneously to entertain and educate. It fulfils a variety of functions. People who visit the British Golf Museum can buy a copy as a souvenir. Golfers with some interest in the history of the game can buy a disc to brush up their knowledge. People with no previous interest in the game can learn something about it. The disc is like the ultimate coffee table book. It provides a resource to which you can return again and again. Golf is a world wide pastime. Translated into Japanese or repackaged for the American market, Great Golf has an enormous potential audience.

When you load Great British Golf into your CD-I player, you see a friendly un-computerish screen. By moving the remote control (or touching the screen at the museum) you reveal a number of buttons. The buttons give you choices: Golf History, Golf Trivia Quiz and Golf Game. Just click on a button or touch the screen and you go straight into the option you have chosen.

Golf History is the serious part of the title, but the approach has a definite lightness of touch. The interest of the subject is amply reflected by the interactive presentation. History stretching back to mediaeval times, memorable games, antique equipment and eccentric players can all be explored in this version of history out of the bunker.

The Golf Trivia Quiz aims to reinforce this lightly acquired knowledge. Questions are graded like the score in golf (you choose between an eagle and bogie to affect your score for a question), and a correct answer is rewarded by a golf competition-like cheer.

Finally the Golf Game allows you to play as a historical character such as Mary Queen of Scots (a doughty golf player) and select a club and a ball. The hole you play is the first on the Old Course at St Andrews, and you have to take into consideration the force with which you hit the ball (how quickly you press the button on the remote control), the direction in which you hit it and the direction of the wind. The result can be anything from a hole in one to the ball plopping ignominiously into the water filled Swilean burn. The animation is hand done, so the game has a friendly rather than an arcade feel.

Great British Golf begins to show the potentiality of CD-I to provide the image quality of video and television and the audience involvement of games, without sacrificing quality. But CD-I is not an arcade game or a video - it a new type of entertainment that combines the best of both worlds.

This Overview should have given you some knowledge of what CD-I is, how it works, and how you go about bringing a title into existence.

If you want to go further, you should contact Philips Interactive Media Systems, who will advise you on equipment and tools. They also offer support, consultancy and a wealth of experience.

FINDING OUT ABOUT CD-I

Now you have read this book, you can find out more about CD-I from the following books:

The CD-I Production Handbook
Aimed at the video and audio production teams involved in making CD-I titles, this book contains detailed examples exploring the concepts and central issues involved.

The CD-I Design Handbook
Aimed at designers with a technical background but no knowledge of CD-I, this book provide detailed, practical coverage of CD-I design, The different stages of CD-I design are richly illustrated with a wealth of examples.

The CD-I Programmer's Handbook
Aimed at CD-I programmers, this book is the standard programming manual on CD-I.

Compact Disc Interactive Media Full Functional Specification (Green Book)
The complete definition of standards for the production of CD-I players and discs. Not for the faint hearted, but contains everything the intending producer needs, and is constantly being updated.

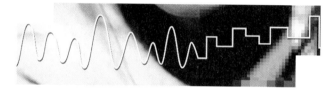

ANALOGUE/DIGITAL

Analogue is the opposite of digital. Analogue methods of recording or displaying information are continuously variable. Digital methods break the information up into small bits (pulses). A watch with smoothly rotating hands is an analogue display because the movement of the hands shows the continuous movement of time. A digital watch slices time up into discrete units. The same distinction applies to analogue and digital methods of recording pictures or sound.

Analogue methods of recording and reproduction tend to cause degradation (eg photocopying); while digital methods are proof against this.

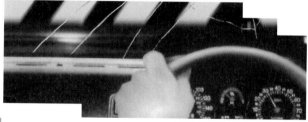

APPLICATION

The use of a technology (such as CD-I) for a specific purpose. For example, a How to Drive CD-I is a training application.

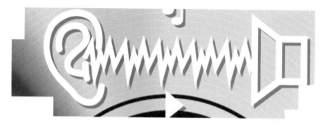

AUDIO QUALITY LEVEL

There are four sound quality levels in CD-I: CD-DA, A, B and C . Level A. This is equivalent to the sort of sound quality when you play a brand new LP on good quality equipment, although without any of the background hiss. You can get two hours of stereo or four hours of mono Level A sound on a CD-I disc.

Level B sound is equivalent to an a first class FM radio broadcast. You can get up to four hours of stereo Level B sound on a CD-I disc.

Level C is more like AM radio received under good conditions. It is completely adequate for speech. You can get about 19 hours of mono Level C audio on a CD-I disc.

AUTHORING

Producing a CD-I application, from concept to master tape. Authoring can also apply more specifically to the computer assisted stages of development such as programming, disc building, emulation and testing.

AUTHORING PLATFORM

A combination of a machine and some software which is used to stitch together and create the links in CD-I programmes. It also allows emulation of the program and may include some graphics facilities for creating menus, text pages etc.

BRANCHING

Moving away from one part of a CD-I programme to another. This is usually in response to user interaction.

CD-I

Stands for Compact Disc Interactive.

CD-DA

Stands for Compact Disc Digital Audio. Uses the compact disc format for storing high quality digital audio.

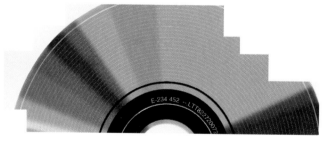

CD-ROM

Compact Disc Read Only Memory. Uses the large storage capacity of a CD disc to store digitally encoded data. This is usually text, and is used in electronic publishing for databases and reference works.

INTRODUCING *CD-I*

131

CD-ROM XA

Compact Disc Read Only Memory Extended Architecture. Uses the large storage capacity of a CD disc to store digitally encoded data. The extended architecture is used to interleave blocks of text, images, music and program data.

COMPRESSION

A technique for reducing the amount of data needed on the disc to store an audio file, an image or sequence of images. For example if an image has large patches which are the same colour, instead of recording the colour of every cell of the picture, the colour is recorded once, along with the run-length (i.e.the number of picture elements following the first with that colour) for each scan line.
There are several different methods of compressing images, which suit different types of image, such as natural images and animated (cartoon) images.
The image is decompressed when the disc is played and it appears on the screen.

DAT

Stands for Digital Audio Tape. A digital audio tape.

DCC

Stands for Digital Compact Cassete.

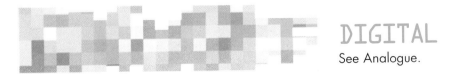

DIGITAL

See Analogue.

EMULATION

The playback process used during development of CD-I titles. The title is developed on the hard disc of the computer. To play it back, you

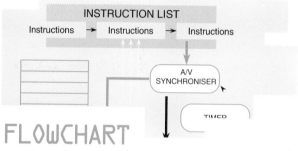

use a program, known as an emulator, which emulates the way the programme would appear if it were actually on a CD-I disc. This is the best way of judging whether the programme is working in the way you intended in the early stages of development.

INSTRUCTION LIST

Instructions → Instructions → Instructions

A/V SYNCHRONISER

TIMED

FLOWCHART

A technique used by computer software designers and others to represent sequences of events in a program using drawings of boxes connected by directional lines.

GREEN BOOK

Two A5 volumes in which all the specifications of the standard for CD-I players and discs are contained. The standard is subscribed to by Philips, Sony, Matsushita and other key manufacturers, and is to CD-I what the Red Book standard was to CD-DA discs.

INTRODUCING **CD-I**

HOTSPOT

An area of the screen which is used to make selections and choices in a CD-I program. Typically, the user uses the remote control to move the pointer on the screen to the hotspot, and clicks a button to make a choice. The hotspot is often a menu button, though it can be some other object, such as an icon.

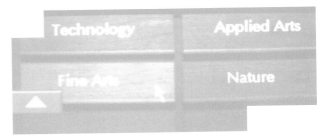

HYPERCARD

An information tool which allows you to store different types of data (still and moving video, graphics, text, music, animation, speech) on cards. The cards are held in stacks and can be accessed in a number of different ways, according to different topics and methods of classification.

HyperCard can be a useful prototyping tool for testing the logic of a CD-I program.

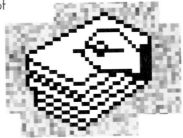

ICON

In computerese, an icon is a small image that stands for something. For example, an hourglass on the screen means that a process is going on and you have to wait. Icons are a useful non-verbal way of showing what is happening or what you need to do. You can use icons with hotspots to enliven the process of making interactive choices for the audience.

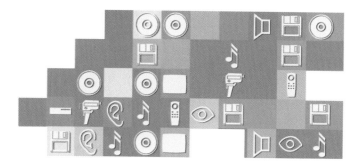

INTERACTIVE MULTIMEDIA

CD-I is a form of interactive multimedia. The combination of interactivity with multimedia, enabling the audience or user to make choices and control the pace, direction and content of a programme.

INTERACTIVITY

Notoriously difficult to define. In multimedia it is the flow of input and output between two systems, one of which is a person and the other of which is the CD-I player and disc. Interactive choices can be used to control pace, direction, content and other aspects of a CD-I programme.

INTERFACE

The interface is the place where a system meets its user. This happens on two levels: first at the hardware level, where the interface is the type of equipment used (eg remote control, keyboard, touch screen); second at the software level, where it is the way the system appears to the user (eg menus, hotspots etc). A well designed interface is essential in making people want to use a programme.

MASTERING

The production of the master disc, from which copies can be made. See Replication.

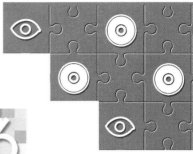

1,048,576

MEGABYTE

One thousand and twenty four kilobytes, or 1,048,576 bytes of data.

MENU

A menu is a list of items on screen from which the user can choose. In an interactive system this can be one way of enabling the user to interact. Each item is accompanied by a button; the user moves the pointer to the button and clicks the remote control to make a choice.

MULTIMEDIA

A medium employing the combination and recombination of elements in a number of individual media, such as video, audio, text and graphics. The process relies upon a computer to bring the bits together and make them into a coherent product.
See also Interactive multimedia.

NATURAL IMAGE

Pictures which are photographic and
appear realistic.

POINTER

The small object on the screen which is moved
around by moving the remote control. Typically, the
pointer is used to point to an item on a menu which is
then selected by clicking a button on the remote
control.

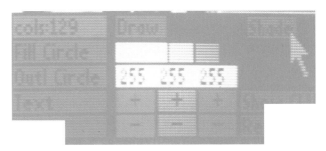

PROGRAM

A computer program controls and organises the contents of the CD-I.

INTRODUCING **CD-I**

PROGRAMME

The CD-I production, like its relatives on radio or television is called a programme (with two Ms).

PROTOTYPING

As with any product, a working model may be the best way of checking whether it is going to work or not. When designing a CD-I disc, certain authoring platforms may be used to construct a simple prototype before production commences in earnest.

REMOTE CONTROL

The physical device which the CD-I user or audience use to control and interact with a programme. Typically, it looks like the remote control for a video player or a television, with the addition of a small joystick. The joystick is used to move the pointer around the screen.

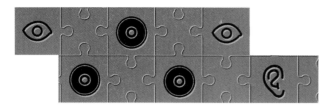

REPLICATION

The manufacturing process by which copies of the master CD-I disc are made.

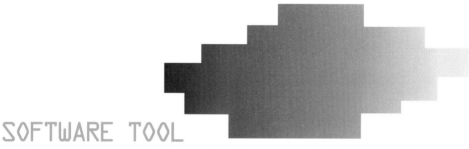

SOFTWARE TOOL

A ready-made piece of software which performs a specified function in the CD-I program - for example, fading from one image to another. The existence of such tools saves having to reinvent the wheel each time a CD-I programme is put together. Software tools are collected into libraries. They can be regarded as the syntax of CD-I.

TOUCH SCREEN

A type of interface in which the user actually touches the screen of the CD-I player to make selections and control the programme. It is ideally suited to point-of-sale and point-of-information systems.

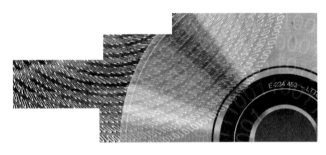

VALIDATION

The process of testing a CD-I disc to make sure that it is ready to be distributed.

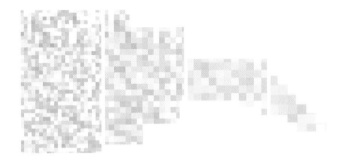

VIDEO QUALITY
(STILLS AND MOTION)

CD-I video pictures can be full screen or partial screen. Partial screen video takes less space on the disc. See Compression.

WORM

Stands for Write Once Read Many. A technique for cutting individual CD-I discs. It is not suitable for mass production, but can be used to make trial discs for testing and validation purposes.

INDEX

INDEX